Life is Strange but
Keep Kindness in Range

Damien Cooper

Life is Strange but
Keep Kindness in Range

Vanguard Press

VANGUARD PAPERBACK

© Copyright 2024
Damien Cooper

The right of Damien Cooper to be identified as author of
this work has been asserted by him in accordance with the
Copyright, Designs and Patents Act 1988.

All Rights Reserved

No reproduction, copy or transmission of this publication
may be made without written permission.
No paragraph of this publication may be reproduced,
copied or transmitted save with the written permission of the
publisher, or in accordance with the provisions
of the Copyright Act 1956 (as amended).

Any person who commits any unauthorised act in relation to
this publication may be liable to criminal
prosecution and civil claims for damages.

A CIP catalogue record for this title is
available from the British Library.

ISBN 978 1 80016 845 9

Vanguard Press is an imprint of
Pegasus Elliot Mackenzie Publishers Ltd.
www.pegasuspublishers.com

First Published in 2024

Vanguard Press
Sheraton House Castle Park
Cambridge England

Printed & Bound in Great Britain

Dedication

This book is a dedication to Peace, Life and Love.

Introduction

An introduction
To my poetry production.
I started reading for my mental health,
I started writing this book of poetry to express myself,
To tell my journey in a creative way,
Because what is the point in going through life and stay,
If you don't use what you go through and feel every day?
Even a daydreamer has something to say,
And this is the only way I know how
to express myself right now.
I am here in life trying, and not just chucking in the towel.
So, this is me.
This is my stamp on society,
Because you can't get someone
If you don't put yourself out and be someone.
To find a love, a partner, a woman, my rock
Who will help me rise in life's creative flock,
Until time has run down the spirit of life's clock?
Drugs to me made a whole lotta sense
In a life so confusing and intense.

That made my life feel so dense
But I take no offence,
Subject of these poems hence.

Finding Colour and Happiness

To the fields of green
With the overwhelming happiness in life that I have seen
This is reality not a dream
That has wiped away the pondering sadness that has been
I know what it's like to feel like you're living in doom
So, when you have a friend that's feeling the sad and gloom
Invite them into the house of peaceful flowers in bloom
And they won't end up in the suicidal depression coffin tomb
Their outlook in life will change to happiness in an instant long term and soon
So don't get in a stoush
Just be as quiet as a mouse
And come and live in my little green house
That has doused my life in a colourful happy haze
In these peaceful relaxing days
Just follow the path of the secret gardens maze
This natural oasis of colours and flowers should have the highest level of praise

Because living life should be enjoyed and be surprisingly amazed.

Living by Night on the Dark Side of Life

Dark eyes in the land of the living dead
Dark eyes up in the midnight skies
Dark eyes bring alive the haunting stories from the dark
 books that I have read
Dark eyes see through all the deceiving dark lies
Dark eyes with a ghost-like face
Dark eyes in this dark, dark place
Dark eyes with dark minds
With all the dark kinds
Where no light shines
When the night of the moonlight brakes
That is when the creatures of the night awake
This is what the transition of the darkness makes
This is just living by night there is no mistake
So, when the darkness of the night falls
Sanity of your mind takes its toll
Heed the phantom of darkness' call
To live this spooky haunting life
When we don't need guns or a knife
Because we who live by night have dark magic power
 of the supernatural

And we fear not even death at all
We live our life just like a Halloween theme
We crave the haunting horror scene
Here in the darkness we live out our life's sin
We go insane with crazy dark eyes and a big grin
Dark eyes in the land of the living dead
Dark eyes up in the midnight skies
Dark eyes bring alive the haunting stories from the dark books that I have read
Dark eyes see through all the deceiving dark lies
Dark eyes with a ghost-like face
Dark eyes in this dark, dark place
Dark eyes with dark minds
With all the dark kinds
Where no light shines
Like being left alone
To be transported to the twilight zone
Some say to be a nomad, an outcast, to be bad to the bone
Some say to be a man to I have grown
We embrace everything about the darkness including the come-downs
Coming down from the power of darkness you become a zombie just a part of the walking dead
Getting chased by thirsty bloodhounds
Who want to shred
From your soul all the purity and light out of you
Until you become purely full of darkness numb and blue.

Mr. Flippy Floppy Wibbly Wobbly Man

I'm slopey dopey good, weird shy
I'm droopy drooly on a good weird down high
My face feels so slopey dopey droopy drooly my nerves and muscles are so relaxed
Right down to the max
I am Mr. Flippy Floppy man with my flippy floppy pants
I am Mr. Wibbly Wobbly man doing my wibbly wobbly dance
Flippy floppy wibbly wobbly my body feels like it is made of jelly
I'm all loosie goosy baby
Just got slopey dopey drooped down
And just flippy floppy wibbly wobbly around
So, call me Mr. Flippy Floppy Wibbly Wobbly man.

(bluie)
Blue Man on the Run

I've got the restless sleepless blues
With my worn-out running shoes
With nothing much to lose
I'm awake through it all to the cold darkness of night
To the misty foggiest morning light
Running farther and farther to the highest of hights
Feeling so pumped and I'm feeling all right
My heart beats too fast
It's like Sonic the Hedgehog's speedy blast
And I know my body won't last
I'm running on fumes
And while everyone stops stares and assumes
I just need another pick-me-up to go-go
I'm bluie on the run and never want to stop and go slow
Like a soldier on a mission and the only objective is to score
This is what they call running blue and going slow is just a bore
And just trying to avoid the inevitable painful rough and raw
That is the crash and burn

And the lesson to learn
Is that either way in the end you'll come to a sudden bang stop
On the floor you'll come to a smack bang hard drop.

(A Psychedelic Angel Chapter) Temporary on Another Planet

In a time of loneliness strange things can happen
She came floating down with a glow wearing white satin
She asked if I wanted to be spiritually free
Grab my hand and come with me
And you will feel a dreamy meditation
So, I reached up without a hesitation
She took me farther then the stars
Even farther then mars
Then in the distance there is an unknown planet I can see
Her home that she's been longing to take me
And she called it the land of ecstasy
Then in the most soothing voice she said say hello
To the strange weird and wonderful planet that is so soft and squishy like one big marshmallow
It's all good here just go with the flow
Of the vibe that's all so groovy and mellow
You'll be welcomed with the gift to be able to unlock your spiritual side

Which would help you to be calm and relaxed on this magical mystery ride
This planet has zero gravity so when your feet have lifted off the soft and squishy ground
And all motions have slowed right down
Then you are at peace and have found
You're truly spiritually at one with this planet
Then she said now you are ready for it to get stranger
And I replied can it
She just reacted with a grin so major
WOW WHOA what's this strange psychedelic sound
That I'm hearing where the volume changes from up to down
Left to right ear echoes through the air
I'm feeling so light soft and squishy floating on clouds like a little Care Bear
This strange magical planet gave me an experience that will stay with me forever
But now it's time to come back down to earth and I will look back on the memory of this as an everlasting treasure.

Working Class Junkie

Alarm clock rings get out of bed
Shake off the slow me down living dead
Spark me up a jump start
To kick, Kick off the working day
It's being productive if I must say
Adapting and using it in the right way
So being a working class junkie is pretty ok
Then come home to rest and daydream away
Expanding my physical and mental growth
Breaking through the barriers of both
It wasn't just a daydream stint
In a basement
With self-entertainment
It was self-achievement
I don't need a congratulation
Just change in the drug Legislation
Start a genuine system through a serious Deliberation
 So we get the progressive recommendation
To the divine spiritual graduation
Peaceful Relaxing vacation
Instead of getting stuck in the aftermath and bench ya

So we can move forward to our next educational adventure.

Where Was I?

I was here there and everywhere, I was neither here nor there, was I even anywhere
Sorry to the people who wanted my life to intertwine into theirs
Just too high and lost trapped inside my own mind to even have a care
Ice cold frozen numb and somewhere neither here nor there, not even anywhere, that's where I was, with no time to spare
The lone journey that I took wasn't the one that they wanted me to take but I knew that this path could not have been one to share
I was on a lonesome journey that was going somewhere, here there and everywhere, but neither here nor there, that wasn't even anywhere, so yet if I was here there and everywhere, but neither here nor there,
Where was I?
I just thought it was best sometimes to be unaware
In a life that has been so unfair
My eyes see
Like a moving timelapse going by at ease

While my mind drifts off and flees
Hearing peoples voice of reason pleas
But still my mind flees into somewhere neither here nor there, not even anywhere, even asking myself where am I?
Thinking to myself in a deep sigh
Maybe it's time to listen to the voices of reason and change my ways
To get my head out of this frozen phase
Until it's too late to be saved
And all that's left is a tombstone with my name engraved
Wake up, wake up death is near
Wake up, wake up I need to get the hell out of here
Where am I, I'm neither here nor there, I'm not even anywhere
Different place different time I was who I was and that was someone who isn't here
It is what it is now and that's what we find so very crystal clear.

Cold Turkey and Getting Clean

Just experiencing life and having some fun
Went too far into the blue and embraced the darkness too much that the damage has already been done
But when I've been living in darkness and despair for too long that I feel the time has come
I'm just so drained I dropped to my knees and can't get back up I feel so heavy like my body weighs a ton
I let it go and stopped fighting against my body and have given in
To give up the devil's crystal to repair and replenish myself from the blood of the devil vampire's sin
There are no alcohol or painkillers this time to ease my pain
This is happening, it's real and if I wasn't already, I think I might be going insane
My mind is scattered like a puzzle putting all the pieces together of my brain
I am no longer numb anymore I feel all the sharp pains in my body and I'm constantly freezing cold
I can never get warm and I'm so alone I just want someone to comfort and to hold

The amount I've had has really effected my body that my insides feel like they have been turned inside - out
I must ask
Not to come near me without a gas mask
Otherwise, there will be casualties at mass
Because I am a toxic chemical hazard full of gas
My senses are in overdrive and have gone haywire everything is so bright and glary
I need to hide away in a quiet dark place because it's so intense I'm hanging on barely
I can hear too much, the sounds are harsh and distorted, too loud and noisy but I'm fighting through it and I'm still alive
My body overheats with the rush of the boiling blood bubbling up my skin I've just got to ignore it and try to cool my body down it will pass, and I will survive.

State Of Mind In The Aftermath

When you're in the prosses of healing
With a lost soul and you can't shake the feeling
There is a marching band in your head
Marching, Marching
The soldier character I can't shed
Marching, marching
The marching band has spread
Marching, Marching
Until the comedy in your life is dead
Marching, Marching
I am over the lies we have been feed
Marching, Marching
Into the aftermath
Waiting for the darkness to pass
Marching, Marching
Into the night
With the bright mind yellow light
Marching, Marching
I thought I was going insane
I just electrified my brain
Running, Running
My mind keeps running

A Man Without the Power of Love

What is a man without love?
Love is the strongest purest strength of all and without it that is a very weak man
For I have never experienced love before
So, when times are hard it's worse without love and comfort so much it really hits you to your core
For I get weaker and weaker as each day has passed
Love can give me the strength to stand tall in this crazy cruel world the power of love is so versatile and vast
Every night I dream oh I dream so for the lover's call
But I always wake up without anybody to love or be loved by, that is why I'm the weakest of all
I want to feel the loving romance I want to feel the comfort of someone and to fall
Into an angel's arms
To free me from this hell I'm in to take me from life's harms
To hold me tight and show me the lover's way
To never let go, to be there for each other and forever stay

To give me the only power and strength in life that matters, love, I too will do the same
Because life and love are not a game
And showing and expressing your love is not lame
Love it is certainly not just a word I realise this because I am a man without love and that is a very weak man.

Vision of My Love

Take a chance
On a date of romance
Nice dinner and a little slow dance
Maybe a drink of the colour of love that of wine
Your dress and shoes are sexy and damn fine
But you my love
You and your body are sweet divine
I will drop my guard for you my love so our hearts can eternally combine
Tell me your heart is mine
To the end of time
They can't hold our love back tonight
We will push back with our love and not fight
And make our love right
They can't hold our love back tonight
We will make love our guiding light
Yes
I want to worship and caress
My goddess
Love is mysterious
But take my love serious
I'm not young and delirious

Trust me I take love at the most serious
Love gets me the most teariest
Only my love can release
My sexual worshipping beast
And I take pleasure in that she would have full control of my leash
I will obey her every command
I will cease and desist and come straight to her at her demand
I am a gentle man
With a gentle hand
I will be her man
And I will forever stick to and stand by her
Where and when, if only I can.

Stuck in Loneliness

Is there a woman out there feeling just like me?
As lonely, lonely as can be
Is there a woman to fill my heart?
Is there a woman to get me out of the dark?
Does she walk out in the rain
Feeling the cold, cold pain
Of loneliness' drain
Life feels like it's stuck in a lonely dark room
Time unnecessary dragged out and wasted in tortured gloom
Tortured for what, what for
Tortured until the thought of living is unsure
Isn't life so cruel
When you always get played for a fool
And get treated like you don't feel at all
Don't you think it's hard for me when I fall
Isn't it sad, isn't it bad?
To be had
I am just a man who's a little bit shy
I am just a man who's just trying to get by
Feeling like a fool, hoping and waiting on a dream that's never going to happen like a diamond in the wind

Like living life as if I have sinned
Don't I deserve love and happiness?
What did I do? I didn't commit an evil crime
I've surrounded my life in darkness with a barricaded wall that seems too big and hard to climb
I've blocked out society for so long that I don't even know how to pick up and start
I need to break down this wall because I know I need love and love is all I need, I'll be romance in art
If only I can find someone who would take that chance on me to read the love and loyalty in my heart
I will never be able to move forward in life without that someone, it's a fact I just can't
Is there a woman out there feeling just like me?
As lonely, lonely as can be
Is there a woman to fill my heart?
Is there a woman to get me out of the dark?
Does she walk out in the rain
Feeling the cold, cold pain
Of loneliness' drain
I will never survive this lonely life consumed by breakdown after breakdown
Depression bound
The cure love cannot be found
Just stuck in the endless cycle of getting nowhere in life and it just keeps on going round and round
Isn't life so cruel
When you always get played for a fool
And get treated like you don't feel at all

Don't you think it's hard for me when I fall
Isn't it sad, isn't it bad?
To be had
I am just a man who's a little bit shy
I am just a man who's just trying to get by.

Stand Proud to be Who You Are

They may call you a rebel
They might try to claim you're the devil
They may call you a punk
They might try to degrade your life to make you feel you have sunk
Don't be someone's fake
Don't just rebel for rebelling's sake
And give into their hate
Don't be someone you're not
Just show them who you are and what you've got
Stay true to yourself, your values, and beliefs
And try to find some peace
In life's griefs
Remember everyone has a bad day
Just don't get stuck and lose your way
And you will be OK
Learn to stand up and fight
For the things in life that really matter and for what is right
Sometimes you may lose and be holding down shattered tears
But never give into your fears

Never let them brainwash you
Into thinking you do not mean anything
Because you do
Never let them break you
Make them look at what hate and ignorance really do when we get told we aren't good enough to be a part of something and get covered up with a lie
We are all different and unique and important little stars that shine brighter than the ones up in the sky
We just need to rise above the hate and ignorance to make a change
Because life is in our hands and kindness is in range
We are who we are and if we can't be that
We need to stand up and object
Because this is everybody's life in effect
Let's all come together
To embrace each other.

A Broken System

Getting used and abused
My life is just a free-for-all
Getting pushed, shoved, and spun around until I fall
Getting so dizzy I can't even find the justice hall
Can someone pick me up and show me some direction?
To the fair-go section
To make the correction
That has been covered up with never a question
They might as well have tossed me in the garbage collection
So, where the bloody hell is the fair-go detection
So, where the bloody hell is the fair-go section
So, where's the freedom of choice
Take a listen to my freedom of voice
They steal my creative material that cannot be taught
These people are the sneakiest invasive spiteful sort
Wasn't there meant to be consent needed that's what I always thought
They just have this attitude that they're too powerful to be caught
But I, I will never be bought
It's only lucky that I haven't taken my own life yet

That is the situation, so what is it that they don't get?
They use my life as a game, that they can put down and
    bet
One life lost
That is the cost
For themselves to profit
Why don't they just grow up and stop it
They say we live in the land of the free
But how can that be?
If your life can be claimed by the entertainment industry
They say we live in the land of opportunity
But how can that be?
If they steal whatever they can see
And hold me back while they take my creativity
So why are they so scared of me?
Being myself in my entirety
And everybody, why can't we
Properly be free?

Set Me Free

Why can't I be free
Why can't you see
Why can't you see the pain you're giving to me?
Why do I even waste my energy?
When I just end up in misery
I just want something genuine and real
Something I can actually feel
Here I lay
Here I lay in a world of crumbling decay
Just take me away
Take me to a better day
I just want a life in authenticity
So why can't you see
Why can't you see the pain you're giving to me?
Just set me free
Stop putting me through such misery
Stop sucking the life out of me
Stop wasting my precious time
Don't leave me bitter and a man past his prime
So why can't I be free
It's like they have got this hold over me
I just want to be free

Tell me now do you see what you are putting me through how can you do somebody so wrong
Can you see it so clear now so how could this happen and why was it dragged out and left so long?
Don't take control and jump the gun
I flow with the beat of my own drum
Don't write down my future as a task
I will pave my own path
Just set me free
Get me out of your misery.

Deprive Me No More

Deprive me not
Of my heart's full fill
Deprive me not
Of life's wondrous thrill
Deprive me not no more
For you have held me back and kept my life at a standstill
Deprive me not
Just because you want to build it up and put it all in one big basket
Deprive me no more
For these are opportunities I should already have so let's just start it
Deprive me not
Of my beauty's loving touch
Deprive me no more
For I have suffered too much
Deprive me not no more
And get me out of your useless spiteful war
Deprive me no more
For I am broken down crying on the floor
Deprive me no more

Just let me go through life's door
Deprive me not
Of my burning love's desire
Deprive me no more
For my heart is on fire.

Trying to Find a Start to Get a Woman's Heart

So, I go back to the drawing board
To try get that right love cord
And find someone new
Like hi how are ya how do ya do
A date can I take you
And would you like to see it through
And get me excited jumping like a bouncing kangaroo
Bring out my sexual beast only to your own private zoo
Waking up alongside of you
Would be like capturing life's most precious view.

The Prowling Fantasy of Love

My oh my love is on the prowl for me
She is on the prowl and looking so damn sexy
My love is on the prowl if you couldn't see
My love is on the prowl, and I am so happy
Because she is on the prowl just for me
My love is not going to throw her love away
Because she is going to throw her love my way
My love is on the prowl, and I am going to be the love
    to stay
And the love to roll around and play
Jumping and bouncing
Scruffily pouncing
So, my love just pounces on me
And I won't let you go astray
Because I want to make you so happy
And I know you would do the same for me
Claw me
Adore me
You are
More to me
Then anyone can see
So, dig deep into me with those claws

Because I am yours
For you I was howling
While for me you were prowling.

The Goddess that I Want to be With

First to step up and progress
If I want to be with my goddess
I want to put the effort in to get a strong reaction
Because the effort I put in would determine the strength of the attraction
I want to put in my all
Just to see her smile
A goddess is not what you might think
So, if you're blinded by ignorance or blink
You will miss the moment in the time of the spiritual link
A goddess is being more than just looks
It's being more than the fairy tales that you read in the books
They're bound
By consideration and empathy in life unkind
And in the darkness of life, you will find
The kindness of a goddess that has shined
And in that kindness, they should be defined
By nothing less
Than a goddess
Make them smile in happiness

And worship and caress
And in doing so feeling privileged to be satisfying a goddess.

(A Psychedelic Angel Chapter)
Coloured Bubble Raindrop

She guided me down with a nice and easy fall
She touched me and soothed my soul
She told me to take a leap and a hop
Into this magic bubble raindrop
She guided me side to side
And took me on another magic mystery ride
And as each motion was moved
The colours merged and grooved
Bumping stretching me back and forth
In a soothing spiritual slow-motion way of course
And made this life that was way too duller
And turned it into a sight of melting misty wavy colour
After sitting and slowing down
The bumping bubble has stood me still on the ground
And then the joyful playful groovy fun
Had very well just begun
When time goes back and resets a scene again
Not quite sure if it's some game
Even so it was a funny little time-warping motion reframe

Through this bubble raindrop I felt the music like I have never felt it before
I feel it I feel it so much more
I felt the mellow cool breeze blowing
And the peace spirit growing
Looking up in the night sky with wonder of the unknowing
With the confusion of life in dissent
The spirits of life have surrounded me with calm and content
And I feel alright, I feel good
I feel happy like I know I should
She cast a sensual lusting desire spell on me
Longing more and more for the love I want to see
In this magic bubble raindrop falling from the sky so free
Feeling the joy of a circus carnival band's glee
Conducted by the clapping monkey and as it claps much faster
I burst out in non-stop continuous laughter
Think again if you thought it ended in disaster
Waking up drowsy the next morning
Then the last part of her trip hit without a warning
Pushing myself up out of bed
The noises and voices in the background that have been said
Stretching and echoing down out of my head
Trying to stretch out of the suction motion
To having a happy peaceful ending notion

Of this psychedelic bubble raindrop potion
To spread the spiritual love in the air
And to spread happiness everywhere
And show love and care.

Love of Marijuana and Music and Love of Love

Marijuana has once again soothed my soul
That has been darkened to black as coal
But still I know love is the missing piece that will make me whole
Marijuana has been my spiritual guidance
That has pushed passed me being uptight and tense
But still, I know only love can push down this wall and fence
Marijuana has made me happy
In this life so crappy
But I still need love and I need it snappy
Marijuana is great
It has freed me of hate
But I still need a romantic date
Because I know love is my fate
Music has soothed my soul
I like all types of music and I love rock and roll
But I know love is life's true goal
Music has been my creative guidance
Music has made this life into some sort of sense
But nothing can compare to love intense

Music has been an energy in my mind that has sparked
    and zapped me
Just give me a beat and make it snappy
But I know love can truly make me happy
There is music for every mood
Music is an art that has been brewed
But love cannot be ignored or shooed
Hear the sweet sound of music in the air
Look around and have a care
Marijuana should be legalised
And should not be demonised
Love should be the priority
In this society
Marijuana is more than just getting high
Music can never die
True love is not a lie
And with all this in mind life is worth a try.

The Notion of Love Lingering

Why does love always linger in wait?
Only for me to be always hoping for a date
Only for me to be stuck alone in loneliness only to masturbate
Why does love always linger in wait?
If only I can find someone to lay with in the magical garden of love
I hope it's not too late
If only I can find someone to lay with in the colourful flowers, green trees, and peaceful vines across the gate
But why does love always linger in wait?
In the suffering sadness of the lonely man's blues
If only I can find someone to lay with and kick off these old man shoes
If only I can find someone to lay with and share our dreams together and have a life we may choose
So why does love always linger in wait?

The Bloke Got Baked

The bloke on his break just wanted to get high
Because he knew there wasn't love close by
Clothesline hangs the bloke dry
With his bong in hand looking at the peaceful sky
Hanging nice in the sun on the clothesline
Hanging the bloke so high airing himself, feeling mother nature's spiritual sign
To a stove simmering cannabutter combine
The bloke did some cooking
To cut back on the chooffing
The bloke is not on yesterday's
Choof, choof
Chooffing train
The bloke cannot go back to those days again
The bloke on his break
Just wanted to make
A batch of brownies and bake
Bake, Bake
Baked, Baked
The bloke got so baked
The bloke baked and ate
Whatever the bloke could find

That would soak up the cannabutter combined
Baked, Baked
Waked, Waked
The bloke got so baked
When he awoke
Outside went the bloke
To have a fresh morning toke
And the bloke got so baked
When he waked and baked
And when the bloke got so baked, he felt his happiness wake
The bloke brewed up some of Mary-Jane's green tea
And a touch of sweetener from a humble bumble bee
Slipping in smooth from Mary-Jane's butter did he
That is the bloke's key
To a mellow afternoon cup of tea
The bloke got himself high
Nah that's a bit of a lie
It was Mary-Jane who swung by
And got the bloke so high
Cutting the bloke some slack
To keep his sanity in tack
So that the bloke can relax and chill back.

Time of Peace

Hey, hey
It's OK
I'm just relaxing through the day
I am an adaptor
Waiting for my next chapter
Where love will be the main factor
It's a time of peace
To rest and feast
Soothe my mind
And leave the negativity behind
Keeping my soul clean
With help of the peaceful green
Staying on track
But looking back
To the experience of the strange
And the experience of the change

Where is My Love Cupid?

Tell me Cupid
Am I always going to get snookered?
I am not stupid
I am not fine
Tell me Cupid where is mine
I wanted to get myself clean
Because I am very romantically keen
But you shot me down hard with your arrow
You carted me off in your wheelbarrow
You keep me aside feeling lonely small and narrow
But I didn't mind
I just wanted a love that is kind
Cupid show me your sign
When do I get mine?

Change Perceptions and Systems

Socially classified outlaw
But you cannot ignore
That it was productive medication
To succeed as my education
Passed a flawed academic system
Take a look and listen
Through reality's brain
See through judgment and have a look again
Through laws and an education system that make you
    go insane
Why do we suffer through school
Feeling like a failure and a fool
There should be different ways of learning that suits you
Because this is what sets your future
We need a genuine drug experience system
With guidance and wisdom
It's all going through life and learning
So cut the red tape there is no need for concerning.